Swimming and Diving

BY M. K. OSBORNE

AMICUS | AMICUS INK

Amicus High Interest is published by Amicus and Amicus Ink
P.O. Box 1329, Mankato, MN 56002
www.amicuspublishing.us

Library of Congress Cataloging-in-Publication Data
Names: Osborne, M. K., author.
Title: Swimming and diving / by M.K. Osborne.
Description: Mankato, Minnesota : Amicus/Amicus Ink, [2020]
 | Series: Summer olympic sports | Audience: Grades: K to
 grade 3. | Includes bibliographical references and index.
Identifiers: LCCN 2019001938 (print) | LCCN 2019013371
 (ebook) | ISBN 9781681518640 (pdf) |
 ISBN 9781681518244 (library binding) |
 ISBN 9781681525525 (pbk.)
Subjects: LCSH: Swimming–Juvenile literature. | Diving–Juvenile
 literature.| Olympics–Juvenile literature.
Classification: LCC GV837.6 (ebook) | LCC GV837.6 .O79
 2020 (print) | DDC 797.2–dc23
LC record available at https://lccn.loc.gov/2019001938

Editor: Wendy Dieker
Designer: Aubrey Harper
Photo Researcher: Shane Freed

Photo Credits: Matt Slocum/AP cover; Francois-Xavier Marit/
AFP/Getty 5, 13; World History Archive/Alamy 6; dpa/
Alamy 9; Nippon News/Alamy 10; Odd Andersen/AFP/Getty
Images 14, 25; Paul J. Sutton/PCN Photography/Alamy 17;
VCG/VCG/Getty 18-19; Matt Dunham/AP 21; PCN Black/
PCN Photography/Alamy 22; EMPICS Sport/AP 26-27; Lukas
Schulze/picture-alliance/dpa/AP Images 29

Printed in the United States of America

HC 10 9 8 7 6 5 4 3 2 1
PB 10 9 8 7 6 5 4 3 2 1

Table of Contents

Going for the Gold

Splash! It's a busy day at the Olympic aquatic center. The world's best swimmers and divers gather every four years at the Summer Games. They race. They dive. They even dance in the water. Each is there with one goal: to win a gold medal.

U.S. gold medalist Michael Phelps creates a storm of bubbles as he begins an Olympic swimming race.

A group of men dive in the pool during the 1932 Olympics.

Q What does FINA stand for?

People have been swimming since the beginning of time. In the first Olympics in 1896, men raced in open water outside. In 1908, **FINA** was formed. This group makes rules for all world water sports, including the Olympics. By 1912, women had events, too. Athletes were diving as well as racing.

 In French, it is short for the Fédération Internationale de Natation, which means International Swimming Federation.

Swimming

Swimming races haven't changed much over the years. The fastest swimmer still wins. Races at early Olympic Games were held outside in open water. Today, most swimmers race in warm pools. Only a few races are in lakes or rivers. The shortest race is one length of the pool, or a distance of 50 meters. The longest race is a 10 kilometer marathon. It takes place in open water.

Judges watch as racers swim to the end of the pool at an Olympic aquatic center.

Masaki Kaneko of Japan does the backstroke at the 2016 Olympics.

Swimmers use four basic strokes in races. Freestyle racers use the front crawl. You'll also see the backstroke. It is like the front crawl, but swimmers race on their backs. Swimmers bob up and down across the pool with the butterfly. The breaststroke is the oldest racing stroke. Each race features one type of stroke. The only exception is the **medley**. You'll see a different stroke every one or two **laps**.

The races in the pool are the most popular events. Swimmers dive off a starting block. They speed to the other end of the pool. In most races, the swimmers do a flip turn at the end. They race back to the start. The first swimmer to touch the wall after finishing the right number of laps is the winner.

Swimmers stay in their lanes
as they race.

Brittany Elmslie of Australia dives in as her teammate touches the wall in the 2016 Olympics.

 Who can be on a relay team?

Some of the most exciting races are the **relays**. This race is for a team of four swimmers. Each one takes a turn doing one or two laps. Here comes the first swimmer! The second one is ready to dive in. And she's off! The fastest team wins the gold medal.

 There are relay teams for just men and just women. New to the 2020 Olympics is a relay for a mixed team of men and women.

The U.S. swimmers are some of the best in the world. They have won more than 550 medals! The next best country is Australia. But they have won only 188 medals in Olympic history. Every four years, swimmers from around the world try to beat the U.S. swimmers. Not very many of them do.

 Which Olympic swimmer has the most medals?

Gold medalist Simone Manuel
of the U.S. starts a 100-meter
race in 2016.

 Michael Phelps. This retired U.S.
swimmer has been to the Olympics
five times and has won 28 medals.

Diving

Diving at the Olympics is about flair. You will see leaps, twists, and flips. Springboard divers jump off a bouncy board. It is 3 meters above the water. Platform divers leap from a stiff board high in the air. It is 10 meters high. That's as tall as a 3-story building!

Cao Yuan of China shows what an Olympic dive looks like.

Judges watch each dive carefully. They give scores based on how well divers flow through each part of the dive. The take-off must be smooth. The flight must be correct. Judges watch the entry into the water. If the splash is small and controlled, a diver gets a good score. In the **synchronized** events, judges make sure the two divers match each other's moves exactly.

 Which diver has the most Olympic medals?

Italian divers Francesca Dallape (left) and Tania Cagnotto earned silver medals for their synchronized dives in 2016.

 Chinese diver Wu Minxia has the most medals. She has also won the most gold medals. Five of her seven Olympic medals are gold.

Chinese diver Lin Yue pulls into a pike position as he flips off the 10-meter platform.

Divers start in the **qualifying** round. They get five or six chances to do a good dive. Judges give each dive a score. The scores are added up. The best divers move to the **semi-final round**. The last round is the **finals**. The top three divers in this round win medals.

Artistic Swimming

One of the most popular sports at the Summer Games is gymnastics. Women's artistic swimming is like gymnastics in the water. These swimmers leap and dive. They spin and twirl. They dance to music. This incredible sport became part of the Summer Olympics in 1984.

 Is artistic swimming the same as synchronized swimming?

The artistic swimming team from Japan does an amazing underwater routine.

 Yes. Until 2017, this sport was called synchronized swimming. It is called artistic swimming now.

You will see **duet** and team artistic swimming events. For duets, two swimmers dance together. They match each other's moves as they swim to the music. Teams have eight members. They do some fantastic dance moves in the water. Swimmers seem to dance on top of the water. They even toss each other into the air.

Lifts show a team's strength and skill in the water.

Swimming to Gold

Water sports are fun to watch. Fans sit on the edge of their seats as hundreds of swimmers and divers compete. Every four years these athletes gather to race, dive, and dance. Who will take home the next gold medal? Turn to the aquatic center pools to find out!

The U.S. 4x100 medley relay team shows off their 2016 gold medals.

Glossary

duet A group of two swimmers.

FINA In French, it is short for the Fédération Internationale de Natation, which means International Swimming Federation; this group makes the rules for international water sports.

finals The last round where the best athletes compete for Olympic medals.

lap One length of the pool, or 50 meters.

medley A swimming race that includes all four strokes in one race.

qualifying The first round of swimming or diving; the winners in a qualifying round move on to the next round.

relay A team race in which each member takes a turn swimming part of the total distance.

semi-final round The second-to-last round in a swimming or diving competition; the winners in a semi-final round go to the final round.

synchronized Done together at the same time.

Read More

Herman, Gail. *What Are the Summer Olympics?* New York: Penguin Random House, 2016.

Nussbaum, Ben. *Showdown: Olympics.* Huntington Beach, Calif.: Teacher Created Materials, 2019.

Rosen, Karen. *Great Moments in Olympic Swimming & Diving.* Minneapolis: Abdo Publishing, 2015.

Websites

Olympic Swimming
www.olympic.org/swimming

Olympic Diving
www.olympic.org/diving

USA Synchronized Swimming
www.teamusa.org/USA-Synchronized-Swimming

Index

About the Author

M. K. Osborne is a children's writer and editor who gets excited about the Olympics, both the Summer and Winter Games, every two years. Osborne pores over stats and figures and medal counts to bring the best stories about the Olympics to young readers.